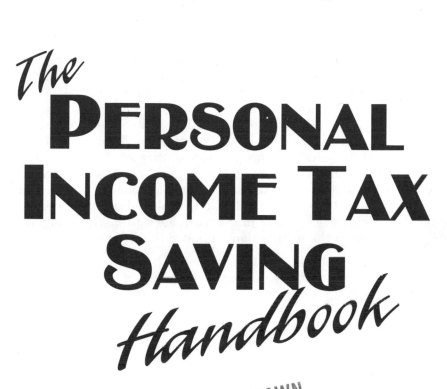

The PERSONAL INCOME TAX SAVING *Handbook*

How To Maximize Your Tax Refund

And Keep More of Your Hard Earned Money

"The avoidance of taxes is the only pursuit that still carries any reward"

— John Maynard Keynes

The information contained in this handbook is for educational purposes only and is not intended for any particular person or circumstance. It is not the intent of the author to attempt to replace any professional advisor. This booklet is intended to assist the user in developing the right questions to ask their advisor(s). A competent tax or financial advisor can serve his or her client better when the client is well informed. Proper tax advice can only be provided through a careful analysis of specific facts as they relate to specific circumstances. The publishers, editors and authors do not assume any responsibility for consequences from any individual's actions predicated upon any information contained in this handbook. One should always be cognizant of the fact that legislative action or inaction can have a significant impact on the application of any of the information contained in this handbook.

Edited by: William B. McAllister
            Certified Public Accountant

Cover Design: Stephen Crane

ISBN: 0-9676087-1-6

Printed in the United States of America

TABLE OF CONTENTS

Page

Chapter I   The Basics
1. Introduction 6
2. Personal Data Record 7
3. General Order and Summary of an Individual Tax Return........................8
4. Sample Tax Planning Worksheet 11
5. Possible Adjustments Toward Adjusted Gross Income 13
6. Certain Tax Aspects of Self Employment 14
7. Moving Tax Breaks 15
8. Gambling Activities Journal..16

Chapter II   Sources and Nature of Income
1. Identify All Your Sources and Nature of Income........................18
2. Interest & Dividend Income Journal 20
3. Tax Aspects of Municipal Bond Purchases 21
4. Capital Gains & Losses Journal....................................22
5. Sample Checklist of Possible Non-Taxable or Excludable Income 23

Chapter III   Real Estate
1. Personal Residence 26
    A. The Tax Advantages of Home Ownership.....................26
    B. Tax Breaks When Selling Your Personal Residence.................27
    C. Home Improvement Record Keeping.........................28
    D. Certain Tax Aspects of a Home Based Business 30
2. Rental (Investment) Property.......................................32
    A. Tax Aspects of Rental Property 32
    B. Examples of Legitimate Tax Shelters 33

Chapter IV   Itemized Deductions
1. Medical Expenses 36
2. Eligible Income Tax and Other Tax Deductions 38
3. Deductible Interest Expenses......................................38
4. Charitable Contribution Deductions 39
5. Casualty & Theft Losses...41
6. Sample Listing of Common Miscellaneous 42
    A. Travel and Entertainment Expenses 44
    B. Auto Expenses...46
    C. Educational Expenses 47
    D. Job Hunting Expenses 48
    E. Alimony Payments/Receipts Journal 49

Chapter V Tax Credits and Tax Strategies

1. Examples of Various Tax Credits 52
2. Family Tax Planning Strategies...54
3. Other Tax Planning Strategies...56
4. Money Saving Investment Strategies 57
5. Income Reducing Strategies 60

Chapter VI Anticipating Audit Matters

1. Substantiate All Information in Your Return 62
2. Checklist of Precautionary Measures 63
3. Know Your Taxpayer Rights..64

Chapter VII Frequently Asked Questions

1. FAQ 68
2. Questions You Want To Ask Your Tax Advisor 74

Chapter VIII Appendix

1. Financial Calendar for Individuals 76
2. Glossary of Terms 77
3. Useful Reference Resources 87
4. Recommended Other Service Providers..89
5. National Taxpayer and Research Organizations 89
6. Develop A Three-Year Plan..91
7. Important Phone Numbers and Addresses 92
8. The All-Purpose Deduction Tracking Form..93
9. Notes 94

CHAPTER I

THE BASICS

1. Introduction
2. Personal Data Record
3. General Order and Summary of an Individual Tax Return
4. Sample Tax Planning Worksheet
5. Possible Adjustments Toward Adjusted Gross Income
6. Certain Tax Aspects of Self Employment
7. Moving Tax Breaks
8. Gambling Activities Journal

Introduction

This resource handbook has been designed to help perform year round tax planning. It is a step by step guide to developing good record keeping habits. This manual can also be used as a quick reference for guidance on various financial matters. The main objective of this handbook is to increase your ability to converse with your tax preparer or financial advisor. Another objective of this workbook is to enhance the benefits of record keeping to ensure you receive all the deductions to which you are entitled; thereby, reducing the amount of tax you pay to the Internal Revenue and related state authorities.

In order to develop a strategy to minimize your taxes, you must first:

1. Determine the sources and nature of your income.
2. Determine the uses of your funds.

After you know where your money comes from and how it is being spent, you can begin to create a tax planning program.

An effective tax saving program must be developed with the cooperation of many parties from a variety of financial fields, and the program must be directed by you on an ongoing basis. The individuals included in a comprehensive tax saving program may include: insurance agents, retirement plan consultants, fringe benefit experts, bankers, brokers, accountants, actuaries, estate planning specialists, attorneys, and others.

General tax strategies would include:

1. Converting taxable income to non taxable as soon as possible.
2. Legally managing your finances to increase income from capital assets while reducing income of an ordinary nature.
3. Deferring or postponing the receipt of income to the subsequent year.
4. Accelerating deductible expenses to the current year.
5. Using tax credits effectively.
6. Establishing a safe harbor estimated tax program.

Maintaining well kept records ensures the opportunity to take advantage of tax avoidance laws. Keep track of your out of pocket expenses and learn to read financial documents so you can learn the costs of managing and investing your money. Tax planning should be annual event.

For individuals using a calendar year, planning activities should be conducted between April 1 and December 25, of the current year. Each Taxpayer may need to address their respective issues at a point in time convenient to their personal needs, the availability of their advisor(s), and the timing of their planned tax saving event. Preplanning an event can make a significant difference in the ultimate financial consequences of that event. An initial consultation could possibly save you thousands of dollars and/or many wasted hours of your precious time.

Personal Data Record

Year: _____

	Taxpayer	Spouse
First Name and Initial	_____	_____
Last Name	_____	_____
Occupation	_____	_____
Social Security #		
Birth date	_____	_____
Address	_____	_____
City/State/Zip	_____	_____
County/Township	_____	_____
Home Phone	_____	_____
Business Phone	_____	_____
Marital Status	_____	_____
Blind/Disabled	_____	_____
Self-Employed	_____	_____
Filing Status:	_____	_____

(Single/Head of Household/Qualifying Widow(er)/Married Filing
Joint/Married Filing Separate)

Dependents:

Name(s)	Age as of 12/31	Social Security Number	Relationship	No. of Months Lived in Your Home

GENERAL ORDER AND SUMMARY OF A BASIC INDIVIDUAL TAX RETURN

Amount

	Gross Income	_____
Less:	Adjustments Toward Adjusted Gross Income	_____
Equals:	Adjusted Gross Income	_____
Less:	Standard Deduction or Itemized Deductions	_____
Less:	Exemptions	_____
Equals:	Taxable Income	_____
	Determine Initial Income Tax	
	Actual Income Tax Liability	_____
Less:	Tax Credits (Subject to Limitations)	_____
Plus:	Other Taxes:	_____
Equals:	Total Tax:	_____
Less:	Actual Taxes Paid	_____
	Earned Income Credit	_____
	Additional Child Tax Credits	_____
	Excess Social Security Tax Paid	_____
	Other Income Tax Payments	_____
Equals:	Balance Due or Refund	

SAMPLE TAX FORM—PAGE 1

Form 1040

Department of the Treasury—Internal Revenue Service

U.S. Individual Income Tax Return **1999** (5) IRS Use Only—Do not write or staple in this space.

For the year Jan. 1–Dec. 31, 1999, or other tax year beginning , 1999, ending , OMB No. 1545-0074

Label
(See instructions on page 18.)

Use the IRS label. Otherwise, please print or type.

L A B E L — H E R E

Your first name and initial | Last name | Your social security number

If a joint return, spouse's first name and initial | Last name | Spouse's social security number

Home address (number and street). If you have a P.O. box, see page 18. | Apt. no.

City, town or post office, state, and ZIP code. If you have a foreign address, see page 18.

▲ **IMPORTANT!** ▲
You **must** enter your SSN(s) above.

Presidential Election Campaign (See page 18.)

Yes | No | **Note.** Checking "Yes" will not change your tax or reduce your refund.

Do you want $3 to go to this fund? . . . .
If a joint return, does your spouse want $3 to go to this fund? . . . .

Filing Status

Check only one box.

1 ☐ Single
2 ☐ Married filing joint return (even if only one had income)
3 ☐ Married filing separate return. Enter spouse's social security no. above and full name here. ▶ ____
4 ☐ Head of household (with qualifying person). (See page 18.) If the qualifying person is a child but not your dependent, enter this child's name here. ▶ ____
5 ☐ Qualifying widow(er) with dependent child (year spouse died ▶ 19). (See page 18.)

Exemptions

If more than six dependents, see page 19.

6a ☐ **Yourself.** If your parent (or someone else) can claim you as a dependent on his or her tax return, **do not** check box 6a. . . . .

b ☐ **Spouse** . . . .

c **Dependents:**

(1) First name Last name	(2) Dependent's social security number	(3) Dependent's relationship to you	(4) ✔ if qualifying child for child tax credit (see page 19)
			☐
			☐
			☐
			☐
			☐
			☐

No. of boxes checked on 6a and 6b ____
No. of your children on 6c who:
• lived with you ____
• did not live with you due to divorce or separation (see page 19) ____
Dependents on 6c not entered above ____
Add numbers entered on lines above ▶ ☐

d Total number of exemptions claimed . . . .

Income

Attach Copy B of your Forms W-2 and W-2G here. Also attach Form(s) 1099-R if tax was withheld.

If you did not get a W-2, see page 20.

Enclose, but do not staple, any payment. Also, please use Form 1040-V.

7 Wages, salaries, tips, etc. Attach Form(s) W-2 . . . . | 7 |
8a **Taxable** interest. Attach Schedule B if required . . . . . . | 8a |
b **Tax-exempt** interest. DO NOT include on line 8a . . . | 8b |
9 Ordinary dividends. Attach Schedule B if required . . . . | 9 |
10 Taxable refunds, credits, or offsets of state and local income taxes (see page 21) . . | 10 |
11 Alimony received . . . . | 11 |
12 Business income or (loss). Attach Schedule C or C-EZ . . . . | 12 |
13 Capital gain or (loss). Attach Schedule D if required. If not required, check here ▶ ☐ | 13 |
14 Other gains or (losses). Attach Form 4797 . . . . | 14 |
15a Total IRA distributions . | 15a | b Taxable amount (see page 22) | 15b |
16a Total pensions and annuities | 16a | b Taxable amount (see page 22) | 16b |
17 Rental real estate, royalties, partnerships, S corporations, trusts, etc. Attach Schedule E | 17 |
18 Farm income or (loss). Attach Schedule F . . . . | 18 |
19 Unemployment compensation . . . . | 19 |
20a Social security benefits . | 20a | b Taxable amount (see page 24) | 20b |
21 Other income. List type and amount (see page 24) . . . . | 21 |
22 Add the amounts in the far right column for lines 7 through 21. This is your **total income** ▶ | 22 |

Adjusted Gross Income

23 IRA deduction (see page 26) . . . . | 23 |
24 Student loan interest deduction (see page 26) . . . . | 24 |
25 Medical savings account deduction. Attach Form 8853 . | 25 |
26 Moving expenses. Attach Form 3903 . . . . . | 26 |
27 One-half of self-employment tax. Attach Schedule SE . | 27 |
28 Self-employed health insurance deduction (see page 28) | 28 |
29 Keogh and self-employed SEP and SIMPLE plans . . | 29 |
30 Penalty on early withdrawal of savings . . . . . | 30 |
31a Alimony paid b Recipient's SSN ▶ ____ | 31a |
32 Add lines 23 through 31a . . . . ▶ | 32 |
33 Subtract line 32 from line 22. This is your **adjusted gross income** . . . . . ▶ | 33 |

For Disclosure, Privacy Act, and Paperwork Reduction Act Notice, see page 54. Cat. No. 11320B Form **1040** (1999)

SAMPLE TAX FORM–PAGE 2

Tax and Credits

34	Amount from line 33 (adjusted gross income)		**34**
35a	Check if: ☐ **You** were 65 or older, ☐ Blind; ☐ **Spouse** was 65 or older, ☐ Blind. Add the number of boxes checked above and enter the total here ▶ 35a		
b	If you are married filing separately and your spouse itemizes deductions or you were a dual-status alien, see page 30 and check here ▶ 35b ☐		

Standard Deduction for Most People

Single: $4,300

Head of household: $6,350

Married filing jointly or Qualifying widow(er): $7,200

Married filing separately: $3,600

36	Enter your **itemized deductions** from Schedule A, line 28, **OR standard deduction** shown on the left. **But** see page 30 to find your standard deduction if you checked any box on line 35a or 35b **or** if someone can claim you as a dependent		**36**
37	Subtract line 36 from line 34		**37**
38	If line 34 is $94,975 or less, multiply $2,750 by the total number of exemptions claimed on line 6d. If line 34 is over $94,975, see the worksheet on page 31 for the amount to enter		**38**
39	**Taxable income.** Subtract line 38 from line 37. If line 38 is more than line 37, enter -0-		**39**
40	**Tax** (see page 31). Check if any tax is from **a** ☐ Form(s) 8814 **b** ☐ Form 4972 ▶		**40**
41	Credit for child and dependent care expenses. Attach Form 2441	**41**	
42	Credit for the elderly or the disabled. Attach Schedule R	**42**	
43	Child tax credit (see page 33)	**43**	
44	Education credits. Attach Form 8863	**44**	
45	Adoption credit. Attach Form 8839	**45**	
46	Foreign tax credit. Attach Form 1116 if required	**46**	
47	Other. Check if from **a** ☐ Form 3800 **b** ☐ Form 8396 **c** ☐ Form 8801 **d** ☐ Form (specify) _____	**47**	
48	Add lines 41 through 47. These are your **total credits**		**48**
49	Subtract line 48 from line 40. If line 48 is more than line 40, enter -0- ▶		**49**

Other Taxes

50	Self-employment tax. Attach Schedule SE		**50**
51	Alternative minimum tax. Attach Form 6251		**51**
52	Social security and Medicare tax on tip income not reported to employer. Attach Form 4137		**52**
53	Tax on IRAs, other retirement plans, and MSAs. Attach Form 5329 if required		**53**
54	Advance earned income credit payments from Form(s) W-2		**54**
55	Household employment taxes. Attach Schedule H		**55**
56	Add lines 49 through 55. This is your **total tax** ▶		**56**

Payments

57	Federal income tax withheld from Forms W-2 and 1099	**57**	
58	1999 estimated tax payments and amount applied from 1998 return	**58**	
59a	**Earned income credit.** Attach Sch. EIC if you have a qualifying child		
b	Nontaxable earned income: amount ▶ _____ and type ▶ _____	**59a**	
60	Additional child tax credit. Attach Form 8812	**60**	
61	Amount paid with request for extension to file (see page 48)	**61**	
62	Excess social security and RRTA tax withheld (see page 48)	**62**	
63	Other payments. Check if from **a** ☐ Form 2439 **b** ☐ Form 4136	**63**	
64	Add lines 57, 58, 59a, and 60 through 63. These are your **total payments** ▶		**64**

Refund

Have it directly deposited! See page 48 and fill in 66b, 66c, and 66d.

65	If line 64 is more than line 56, subtract line 56 from line 64. This is the amount you **OVERPAID**		**65**
66a	Amount of line 65 you want **REFUNDED TO YOU** ▶		**66a**
▶ **b**	Routing number ☐☐☐☐☐☐☐☐☐ ▶ **c** Type: ☐ Checking ☐ Savings		
▶ **d**	Account number ☐☐☐☐☐☐☐☐☐☐☐☐☐☐☐☐☐		
67	Amount of line 65 you want **APPLIED TO YOUR 2000 ESTIMATED TAX** ▶ 67		

Amount You Owe

68	If line 56 is more than line 64, subtract line 64 from line 56. This is the **AMOUNT YOU OWE.** For details on how to pay, see page 49 ▶		**68**
69	Estimated tax penalty. Also include on line 68	69	

Sign Here

Joint return? See page 18.

Keep a copy for your records.

Under penalties of perjury, I declare that I have examined this return and accompanying schedules and statements, and to the best of my knowledge and belief, they are true, correct, and complete. Declaration of preparer (other than taxpayer) is based on all information of which preparer has any knowledge.

Your signature	Date	Your occupation	Daytime telephone number (optional) ( )
▶ Spouse's signature. If a joint return, BOTH must sign.	Date	Spouse's occupation	

Paid Preparer's Use Only

Preparer's signature ▶	Date	Check if self-employed ☐	Preparer's SSN or PTIN
Firm's name (or yours if self-employed) and address ▶		EIN	
		ZIP code	

Form **1040** (1999)

SAMPLE TAX PLANNING WORKSHEET

This worksheet has been designed for estimation purposes only, and should only be used as a starting point for discussions with your tax preparer.

Income   Year _____

1. Salaries from W-2 Form   _____
2. Dividend Income   _____
3. Interest Income   _____
4. Net Business Income/(Loss)   _____
5. Net Capital Gains   _____
6. Other Gains/(Losses)   _____
7. Passive Income/(Losses)   _____
8. Other Income   _____
9. Total Income (Sum of lines 1 thru 8)   _____

Adjustments

10. Alimony Paid   _____
11. Keogh or SEP Plan Contributions   _____
12. Deductible IRA Contributions   _____
13. Moving Expenses   _____
14. Other Adjustments   _____
    One Half of Self-Employment Tax   _____
    Self-Employed Health
      Insurance Deduction (60%)   _____
    Student Loan Interest (Max. $1,500)_____
15. Total Adjustments (Sum of lines 10 thru 14)   _____
16. Adjusted Gross Income (AGI)
    (Subtract line 15 from line 9)   ==================

Deductions

17. Medical and Dental Expenses
    (Excess over 7.5% of line 16) _____

18. State and Local Income Taxes _____

19. Real Estate Taxes _____

20. Personal Property Taxes _____

21. Home Mortgage Interest _____

22. Investment Interest _____

23. Charitable Contributions _____

24. Casualty or Theft Losses
    (Excess over $100 plus 10% of line 16) _____

25. Miscellaneous Expenses
    (Excess over 2% of line 16) _____

26. Total Deductions
    Sum of lines 17 thru 25 Less 3% of
    (line 16—$117,950) or the standard deduction,
    if greater. _____

27. Personal Exemptions _____

28. Regular Taxable Income
    (Subtract lines 26 and 27 from line 16) _____

29. Regular Tax (From the Tax Tables) _____

30. Tax Credits _____

31. Regular Tax (Net) (Subtract line 30 from line 29) _____

32. Alternate Minimum Tax _____

33. Other Taxes (Self Employment Tax, etc.) _____

34. Total Tax Due (Sum of lines 31, 32 and 33) _____

35. Total Withholding & Estimated Tax Payments _____

36. Balance Due or (Refund)
    (Subtract line 35 from line 34) _____

Possible Adjustments Toward Adjusted Gross Income

Even if you elect not to itemize your deductions, some of the following deductions may be available to you.

	Amount
• Alimony Paid	_____
• Contributions to an IRA, SEP, Keogh Plan or Simple Plan	_____
• A Portion of Health Insurance Costs by the self-employed	_____
• Some Student Loan Interest	_____
• Contributions to a Medical Savings Account (MSA)	_____
• Limited Moving Expenses (If Job Related)	_____
• One-half of the Self-employment Tax Paid.	_____
• Imposed Penalties for early withdrawal of savings.	_____
• Forestation/Reforestation Amortization Expense	_____
• Self-employed Net Operating Loss Deduction	_____
• Short or Long-Term Capital Loss Carryovers	_____
• Losses on Involuntary Conversions	_____
• Investment Losses (Worthless Bonds & Stocks)	_____
• Non-Business Bad Debts	_____
• Gambling Expenses	_____

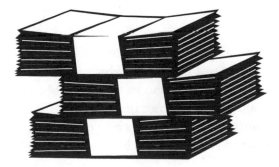

CERTAIN TAX ASPECTS OF SELF-EMPLOYMENT...

If you own an unincorporated business or you are an S Corporation Shareholder, business losses may be deductible on your personal income tax return.

Notes

- Self-employed individuals are allowed to deduct prescribed amounts of their health insurance payments as an adjustment toward AGI. _____

- You may be able to deduct 100% of your health insurance costs as a trade or business expense. _____

- You can remove in excess of $4,600 per eligible child, when they are employed by their parent's sole proprietorship. _____

- Your business losses are generally deductible against your other sources of income. _____

- One half of your self-employment taxes are deductible as a trade or business expense. _____

- Your income is not subject to withholding tax. _____

- All of the following types of business expenses may be deductible.

  - Automobile _____   - Bad debts _____
  - Travel _____   - Casualty Losses _____
  - Entertainment _____   - Inventory Losses _____
  - Meals _____   - Capital Losses _____
  - Home Office _____   - Net Operating Losses _____

- You can establish a qualified retirement Keogh Plan or a Simplified Employee Plan (SEP), which allows amounts contributed to the plan to be deductible at the time of contribution, and are not treated as income until the amounts are withdrawn, and you are possibly in a lower tax bracket. (Just do so before December 31.) _____

- Certain family members who work for the parent's sole proprietor may be exempt from state and federal unemployment taxes. _____

- Family members under the age of 18, who work for a parent's sole proprietorship are exempt from social security taxes. _____

- In 1998 take advantage of Section 179 expensing, and expense up to $18,500 in purchases of qualified property placed in service, rather than depreciating it over an extended period of time. _____

- Unused Net Operating Losses can be carried back two years or carried forward for as long as 20 tax years. _____

MOVING TAX BREAKS

If you moved to a new home because you got a new full-time job, that is at least 50 miles from your old employer, you are eligible for some tax breaks on the expenses of the move.

Notes

- Packing/Supplies Costs _____

- Travel Costs _____

- Transportation/Moving Costs _____

- Lodging Costs _____

- Temporary Furniture Storage Costs _____

- Moving Insurance Costs _____

- Connecting/Disconnecting Utilities _____

- Shipping Car/Pets _____

- Miscellaneous _____

    Total Moving Expenses: _____

    Amount Reimbursed by Employer (–) _____

    Tax Deductible Moving Expenses (=) _____

GAMBLING ACTIVITIES JOURNAL

Notes:

You must first qualify under IRS rules as a professional gambler.

Also keep receipts for ticket purchases, as well as those for travel costs such as lodging and airfare for a trip to a casino.

Date of Gambling	Location of Gambling	Wager Amount	Type of Gambling	Winnings/ (Losses)

Net Position: _____

CHAPTER II

SOURCES & NATURE OF INCOME

1. Identify All Your Sources and Nature of Income
2. Interest & Dividend Income Journal
3. Tax Aspects of Municipal Bond Purchases
4. Capital Gains & Losses Journal
5. Checklist of Possible Non Taxable or Excludable Income

IDENTIFY ALL YOUR SOURCES OF INCOME

Income Source	Taxable	Non Taxable	
Wages/Salaries (W-2 Forms)			
Dividends			
Interest Income			
Alimony Received			
Self Employed Income or Loss			
Farm Income or Loss			
Other Capital Gains & Losses			
Distributions from Retirement Plans or Accounts			
Income from Rental Properties			
Directors Fees Received			
Royalty Income			
Annuity Income			
Social Security Income			
Income from Trusts or Estates			
Income from Partnership or S Corporation(s)			
Unemployment Compensation			
Jury Duty Fee			
Tips and Gratuities			
Awards and Prizes			
Gambling Income			
Commissions & Bonuses			
Foreign Source Income			
Non Compete Income			
Sales of Securities & Property			
Sales of Real Estate			
Other Income			
Totals:			

Note: Refer to Sample Checklist of Non Taxable and Excludable Items

18

Not Sure	Subject To Self Employment Tax	Capital Gains or Losses

at the end of this chapter.

INTEREST AND DIVIDEND INCOME JOURNAL

Interest Income:

Source Codes: MB = Municipal Bonds   IN = Installment Sales
US = US Bonds   TE = Tax Exempt
MF = Mortgage Financed by Seller

Name of Payer	Interest Amount	Exempt Amount	Source Code

Dividend Income:

Name of Payer	Gross Dividend	Ordinary Dividend	Capital Gain	Non-Taxable Amount	State Exempt

TAX ASPECTS OF MUNICIPAL BOND PURCHASES...

The income from municipal bonds is exempt from federal taxes. For example, for someone in the 28% federal tax bracket, the 5.1% yield has a taxable equivalent yield of 7.1%. In other words, you need to get a 7.1% yield from a taxable bond to equal the 5.1% payout of the municipal bond. Consequently, higher personal income tax rates dramatically increase the appeal of tax-exempt municipal bonds, and mutual funds that invest in these types of bonds.

Additionally, if you buy a bond issued locally within your own state, you can also usually shield the income from your state and local income taxes.

For extra safety, you can buy insured munis or prerefunded munis backed by Treasury Bonds.

You must decide to either buy individual municipal bond issues directly from a broker or you can purchase shares in a mutual fund, that owns a diversified portfolio of municipal bonds.

Direct Purchase:

Disadvantages: Individual Municipal bonds are sold in increments of $5,000, and a $25,000 minimum investment is needed to get the best price. You must also consider the rare occurrence of bankruptcy by the municipality.

Advantages: They are virtually guaranteed to give back your initial investment upon maturity.

Municipal Fund Purchase:

Disadvantage: You are not guaranteed that your principal will be returned.

Advantage: You can make as little as a $1,000 investment.

Suggested Selection Criteria:

Choose Municipal Mutual Funds using the following criteria:
- Intermediate-term issues with average maturities of 10 years or less
- No front-end load
- No back-end/deferred load
- An annual expense ratio of 1.0% or lower
- An Average Portfolio Quality of AA or better
- A minimum initial investment requirement that matches your resources.

CAPITAL GAINS AND LOSSES JOURNAL

Date Acquired	Asset Description	No. of Shares	Fees/ Commission	Cost or Basis	Sale Date	Sale Price

CHECKLIST OF POSSIBLE NONTAXABLE OR EXCLUDABLE INCOME

The following list represents income which may be either partly or completely nontaxable to you, depending if certain conditions are met. Check those that apply to your situation.

Source of Nontaxable Income   Amount

- Any Return of a previously incurred cost. (Refunds) _____
- No-Additional Cost Service provided by employer. _____
- Accident and Health Insurance Premiums paid by your employer _____
- Adoptive Parent's Payments from a state agency. _____
- Allotment paid to serviceman's dependent _____
- Lump Sum Alimony or Non-periodic Payments (Divorce Settlement) _____
- Annuities return of your investment. _____
- Bequests and Devises _____
- Board & Lodging furnished by an employer (for convenience of employer) _____
- Bond Interest received on certain obligations of state or local governments. _____
- Return of Capital _____
- Carpool Receipts _____
- Casualty Insurance Proceeds _____
- Child Care provided by employer _____
- Child Support Payments/Assistance _____
- Combat Pay up to a certain limit _____
- Damages resulting from certain types of suits. _____
- Disability Benefits other than for loss of wages. _____
- Dividend Distributions which reduce the cost basis of your stock. _____
- Education Course Expenses required by your employer _____
- Employee Death Benefits _____
- Qualified Employee Discounts _____
- Employee Fringe Benefits _____
- On-site Athletic Facility Usage _____
- Endowment Policy proceeds until cost is recovered _____
- Insurance Dividends from mutual insurance companies _____
- VA Insurance Dividends _____
- Federal Income Tax Refunds _____
- Fellowship Grants _____
- Foreign Earned Income _____

Source of Nontaxable Income   Amount

- Foster Care Payments from government agencies _____
- Frequent Flyer Bonus   _____
- Gain on Sale of personal residence   _____
- Gifts received from employer during holidays   _____
- Group Term Life Insurance Premiums   _____
- Group Legal Services Plans   _____
- Health & Welfare Payments   _____
- Health Insurance Proceeds   _____
- Home Energy Assistance Payments   _____
- Inheritances   _____
- Life Insurance Proceeds   _____
- Loans   _____
- On-site Lodging to carry out the duties of your job _____
- Marriage Settlements   _____
- Moving Expenses Paid   _____
- Municipal Bond Interest   _____
- Mutual Funds Dividends that are a return of capital _____
- Nobel Prize or Pulitzer Award   _____
- Parsonage Allowances   _____
- Pension Plan Contributions by employer to qualified plan _____
- Qualified Transportation provided by your employer _____
- Rebates of Cash on purchases   _____
- Reimbursement for expenses paid for your employer _____
- Scholarship Grants   _____
- Security Deposit paid to landlord   _____
- Sickness & Injury Benefits equivalent to workman's compensation _____
- Social Security Benefits   _____
- State Tax Refunds   _____
- Stock Option to buy employer's stock   _____
- Tax Exempt Interest   _____
- Tax-free Exchanges of Property   _____
- Tools from your employer needed in your line of work _____
- Tuition paid by employer   _____
- Utility Company Rebates for installing energy conservation devices _____
- Veteran Benefits   _____
- Unemployment Compensation   _____
- Welfare Benefits   _____
- Working Condition Fringe Benefits   _____
- Workmen's Compensation   _____

Totals: _____

CHAPTER III

REAL ESTATE

1. Personal Residence

    A. The Tax Advantages of Home Ownership

    B. Tax Breaks When Selling Your Personal Residence

    C. Home Improvement Record Keeping

    D. Certain Tax Aspects of a Home Based Business

2. Rental (Investment) Property

    A. Tax Aspects of Rental Property

    B. Examples of Legitimate Tax Shelters

"Home Sweet Home"

THE TAX ADVANTAGES OF HOME OWNERSHIP

Your home is probably your most substantial asset and can provide your biggest tax shelter. Do everything possible to maximize your after-tax return and allowable deductions from this key investment.

The Key Housing Tax Breaks are as follows:

Notes

- The primary benefit of home ownership is the mortgage interest deduction. You can deduct the interest on up to $1 million of an acquisition mortgage on your principal residence, and/or

  vacation home. _____

- You can deduct the interest on up to $100,000 of a Home Equity Loan, assuming the loan does not exceed the fair market value of your home. _____

- The points you paid on the original mortgage may also be deductible, if you did not use a mortgage broker, and the loan is used to buy or improve your principal residence and is secured by that home. A broker typically charges a broker's fee or commission, and these are not deductible. _____

- Points on refinanced mortgages are also deductible, but they must be amortized over the life of the loan. _____

- Local property taxes are fully deductible in the year in which they are paid. _____

- Home Improvement Loan Interest _____

- Home Improvement Loan Points Paid (To Be Amortized) _____

Notes:

It is very important to consolidate and trade personal debt for home mortgage debt, because the interest expense on mortgage debt or a home equity loan is deductible, while consumer or personal interest is not, and home equity loans are usually offered at a 'preferred rate'.

Interest on borrowings of up to $100,000 secured by your personal residence is usually fully deductible, regardless of how the proceeds are used.

Try to establish your domicile or permanent residence in a state which has no state income tax.

SELLING YOUR HOME TAX BREAKS

The following are examples of expenses of the sale, and they are deductible from your gain on the sale. Your taxable capital gain is the difference between your house selling price and your cost basis, which is what you paid for the house plus any capital improvements.

Notes

- Broker Sales Commission _____
- Legal Fees _____
- Administrative Costs _____
- Inspection Fees _____
- Advertising _____
- Fix-up Expenses for Sale _____
- Miscellaneous _____

Total Expenses of Sale: _____

You can now exclude a maximum of $250,000 ($500,000 if married and filing jointly) when you sell your home for a gain, if you:

- Used the house as your principal residence for a minimum of 2 years.
- You owned the property for at least 2 years.
- It has been at least 2 years since you took this exclusion.

Property Sale Capital Gain Calculation:

- Selling Price: _____
- Total Expenses of Sale: (–) _____
- Amount Realized (=) _____
- Adjusted Cost Basis (–) _____

  Includes: Purchase Price _____
  Improvement Costs _____
  Acquisition Costs _____

- •Net Gain Realized (=) _____

RECORD OF HOME IMPROVEMENTS

Home Improvements can help to increase your cost basis if they meet any of the following criteria:

- Materially add to the value of your home.
- Considerably prolong its useful life.
- Adapt the home to a new use.

Instruction: Keep this form for your records and keep receipts or other proof of improvements to reduce the amount of gain that is taxable when you sell your home by adjusting the cost basis.

Type of Improvement	Date	Amount	Notes

Additions:

Bedroom

Bathroom

Deck/Patio

Garage

Porch

Storage Shed

Fireplace

Other

Lawn and Grounds:

Landscaping

Driveway

Walkway

Fences

Retaining Wall

Sprinkler System

Swimming Pool

Exterior Lighting

Other

Electrical:

Lighting Fixtures

Wiring Upgrades

Circuit Breaker Panel

Other

Type of Improvement	Date	Amount	Notes

Plumbing:

Water Heater			
Soft Water System			
Filtration System			
Other			

Insulation:

Attic			
Walls/Floors			
Pipes/Duct Work			

Communications:

Satellite Dish			
Intercom			
Security System			
Other			

Interior Improvements

Built-in Appliances			
Kitchen Modernization			
Bedroom Modernization			
Flooring			
Other			

Miscellaneous:

Storm Windows/Doors			
Roof			
Central Vacuum			
Other			

Totals:

Notes: Attach a copy of your settlement statement.

Closing Date: _____

Improvements are considered to be capital expenditures and must be depreciated over time.

THE TAX ADVANTAGES OF A HOME-BASED BUSINESS

Beginning in 1999, the home office deduction has been expanded significantly. A deduction is now allowed if you use your home office regularly to conduct administrative or management activities for your trade or business, as long as there is no other fixed location where you conduct such substantial activities, and you use your separate home office space regularly and exclusively for business purposes. You cannot mix business and personal uses and take the deduction.

Caution: This portion will not be eligible for exclusion on sale.

Also, remember that your home business does not have to make money for you to take any related business deductions. But, you do have to show the intent to make a profit.

Calculating Your Deduction (Discuss with your Tax Advisor)

- **First, determine the Percentage of Business Use.**

  –The number of square feet exclusively used for
   your home business: _____

  –Divided by your home's total square footage: _____

  –Equals the Percentage of Business Use: _____

- **If You Rent.**

  –Your Annual Rent Payment: _____

  –Times Percentage of Business Use: _____

  –Equals Home Office Deduction: _____

- **If You Own Your Home You Can Take a Deduction for Depreciation.**

  –For buildings bought before 1994, this period is 27.5 years; for buildings bought since then, it is 39 years.

  –If you bought the property after 1987, you must deduct the same amount each year, this is known as straight-line depreciation. For property bought earlier, you can use accelerated depreciation and take larger deductions in the first few years.

  –You must also determine the values of the building and the land separately. An allocation of 80% to structure and 20% to land is common in most of the country.

- **Depreciation Calculations:**

  House Purchase Price: _____

  Times: Structure Value Percentage: _____

  Equals: Depreciable Structure Amount: _____

  Divided By: Number of Depreciable Years _____

  Equals: Allowable Depreciation per year _____

  Times: Percentage of Business Use _____

  Equals: Per Year Deduction for Home Office _____

	Total Cost	Bus. Expense

Direct Expenses:

- Painting of Office Space _____
- Repairs to Office Space _____
- Computer Accelerated Depreciation _____
- Office Furniture _____

Indirect Expenses:

Multiply Total Cost by Business Percentage Use

	Total Cost	Bus. Expense
• Real Estate Taxes:	_____	_____
• Home Mortgage Interest:	_____	_____
• Utilities	_____	_____
• Security System:	_____	_____
• Casualty Losses:	_____	_____
• Rent	_____	_____
• Insurance	_____	_____
• Home Repairs	_____	_____
• Depreciation	_____	_____
• Snow Removal	_____	_____
• Cleaning	_____	_____

Totals: _____ _____

Notes:

Turn your home into a tax-free income producing vehicle through the use of a 'reverse mortgage'. (Caution: Use extreme caution before using a reverse mortgage)

Direct expenses benefit only the business portion of your home, and you can deduct 100% of their cost.

Indirect expenses are those that cannot be attributed to a particular area of the house and, therefore, benefit both the business and personal areas. They must be multiplied by your business use percentage.

Home Office deductions are limited in the current year by your gross income earned in that home office, but you can carry forward unused deductions indefinitely, if you have future year gross income to offset it.

THE TAX BENEFITS OF RENTAL PROPERTIES

If you rent your second residence, you may reduce your taxable income further through the deduction of the following types of rental expenses:

Notes

- Repairs & Maintenance _____
- Advertising _____
- Janitorial and Maid Service _____
- Rental of Equipment _____
- Utilities _____
- Fire and Liability Insurance _____
- Property Taxes _____
- Mortgage Interest _____
- Commissions _____
- Management Fees _____
- Travel & Transportation Expenses _____
- Auto Expenses _____
- Depreciation of House _____
- Depreciation of Furniture/Fixtures _____
- Accounting/Bookkeeping Expenses _____

Notes:

If you believe your house will decline in value before you sell it, consider converting it into a rental property, so that the loss may be deductible.

Caution: Be careful not to lose your right to exclude the gain on sale of personal residence.

You may deduct rental expenses on your property during the period in which it was not being rented, as long as you can document the fact that you were actively trying to rent it out.

You can own a dwelling for both rental use and personal use, as long as you divide your expenses proportionately, using the following formula: Expenses times Rental Days divided by Total Days.

If a residence is rented out for fewer than 15 days during the taxable year, the rental income is not taxable.

If you give a remainder interest in a personal residence or a farm to a qualified charity, the present value of the remainder interest is currently deductible as a charitable contribution.

When you die, the increased value of your home is not subject to income tax. Your heir's basis in your home becomes the fair market value of your home at the time of your death.

Your tax liability from the sale of real property can be deferred if you exchange the property for similar property.

If you buy an appliance for your rental house, it is classified as a seven-year property, under the Modified Accelerated Cost Recovery System (MACRS).

EXAMPLES OF LEGITIMATE TAX SHELTERS:

Notes

- Rental Real Estate Properties provide a good tax shelter, if you are willing to actively manage the property, because of the depreciation and mortgage interest expenses. _____
- Primary and Second Home Investments _____
- Low-Income Housing Investments _____
- Rehabilitation of Older Buildings _____
- Rehabilitation of Certified Historic Structures _____
- Individual Retirement Accounts (IRAs) _____
- Employer Sponsored Retirement Plans _____
- Small Business Stock Gain Exclusions _____
- Designated Empowerment Zone Tax Advantages _____
- Working Interest in Oil & Gas Properties _____
- Annuity Contracts _____
- Whole Life Insurance Plans _____
- Start Your Own Business from Your Home _____

Notes:

One of the most effective ways to reduce your taxes is to start your own business. This enables you to convert many personal expenses into deductible business expenses. You must, however, show a 'profit motive' so that your expenses are allowable as tax deductions.

If your adjusted gross income is under $150,000, you may be able to deduct up to $25,000 in losses each year from investment property that you actively manage.

It may be better to hold appreciated investment property until you die, because the tax obligations for asset appreciation are wiped out at death. (Estate Planning can be very beneficial).

Tax-free exchanges of investment property (not personal residences) can extend the tax benefits because you basically exchange one piece of investment property for another without owing any taxes.

The alternative to selling investment property and paying capital gains is to refinance and receive tax-free cash and interest deductions.

The appeal of oil and gas investing is that most startup costs involved in drilling for oil and gas can be deducted immediately, and, if your drilling is successful, the proceeds may be sheltered by the depletion allowance.

LEARNING MORE ABOUT TAX SHELTERS...

One of the following three elements are common to most tax shelters:

- **Income Deferral**

   Deductions are accelerated in the early years in order to reduce tax liability.

- **Leverage**

   Borrowed funds are used in a taxpayer's investments to pay the expenses for which accelerated deductions, such as investment interest expense, are received.

- **Income Conversion**

   Involves the conversion of ordinary income to capital gains at the time of asset disposition and the realization of a lower tax rate.

Legitimate tax shelters are substantial investments that exist to reduce taxes fairly, and to produce income with some degree of risk. They often involve losses to produce future gains.

Generally, the amount of your deductions or losses from most activities is limited to the amount that you have 'at risk'. You must also show evidence of an intent to make a profit.

An abusive tax shelter exists solely to reduce taxes unrealistically, and promoters claim there is little risk involved. Additionally, an abusive tax shelter uses inflated tax savings based on large write-offs and credits, and is often out of proportion to your investment. These types of tax shelters are usually too good to be true.

In comparing the tax shelter investment against other investment alternatives, you should determine the actual profit potential, which means measuring the potential after-tax return against the after-tax cost. Incorporate the following steps into your analysis:

- Evaluate the assumptions upon which forecasted projections have been based.
- Study the possibility of and conditions for additional assessments.
- Examine the promoter's past history and track record.
- Evaluate the front-end fees and commissions of the general partner.
- Evaluate the realism of the timetable for receiving the expected yields.
- Evaluate the impact of potential phantom income.

CHAPTER IV

ITEMIZED DEDUCTIONS

1. Medical Expenses

2. Eligible Income Tax and Other Tax Deductions

3. Deductible Interest Expenses

4. Charitable Contribution Deductions

5. Casualty & Theft Losses

6. Listing of Common Itemized Miscellaneous Deductions

7. Job Hunting Expense Journal

KEEP TRACK OF YOUR MEDICAL EXPENSES

In order to deduct your medical expenses, the total of your unreimbursed medical expenses must be more than 7.5% of your Adjusted Gross Income.

Notes:

You can use a standard rate of 10 cents per mile when you use your car for medical reasons.

When seeking medical care away from home, you can deduct lodging expenses of up to $50 per night per individual as a medical expense.

If you make a medically related capital improvement to your home, such as an elevator, you can deduct that portion of the expenditure which does not add value to your property.

You can claim medical expenses you paid for your parents if you provide more than half of their support.

Less commonly known types of medical expenses:

- Acupuncture
- Blood Sugar tests
- Long-term Care Facilities
- Hospitalization Expenses
- Vasectomy
- Artificial Teeth
- Medical Aid Rental
- Nurses (Room & Board)
- X-rays
- Hearing Aids & Supplies
- Smoking Cessation Programs
- Elastic Stockings
- Medical or Oxygen Equipment
- Nursing Home Medical Care
- Special Schooling for handicapped persons
- Abortion
- Long-term Care Insurance Premiums
- Medicare Part B Service Payments
- Ambulance Service
- Lab Fees
- Eye Glasses/Contact Lenses

– Anything prescribed by a doctor for medical purposes:

- Reclining Chair
- Whirlpool Bathtub
- Dehumidifier
- Special Foods/Diets
- Tutoring Fees
- Prescriptions & Drugs
- Alcoholism & Drug Abuse Treatment
- Childbirth Preparation Classes
- Special Mattress
- Central Air Conditioning
- Swimming Pool
- Vitamins
- Paint Removal
- Contraceptives

MEDICAL EXPENSE JOURNAL

Medical Expense Codes: D = Diagnosis   T = Installment Sales
    C = Cure   P = Prevention
    M = Mitigation   I = Insurance Premiums

Date	Type of Expense/ Reason	Location	Total Cost	Percent Reimbursed	Actual Expense

ELIGIBLE INCOME TAX AND OTHER TAX DEDUCTIONS

The following list of eligible income tax deductions is subject to certain limitations and types of taxes:

A. State Income Taxes _____

B. Local Income Taxes _____

C. Foreign Income Taxes _____

D. State and Local Property Taxes _____

E. Real Property Taxes _____

F. Other Taxes _____

DEDUCTIBLE INTEREST EXPENSES

The following list of deductible interest expenses is subject to certain limitations and the nature of the interest paid:

A. Mortgage Interest (Principal Residence) _____

B. Mortgage Interest (Second Home) _____

C. New Mortgage Points _____

D. Home Equity Loan Interest _____

E. Home Improvement Loan Interest _____

F. Mortgage Prepayment Penalties _____

G. Margin Account Interest _____

H. Investment Interest Expenses _____

CHARITABLE CONTRIBUTION DEDUCTIONS...

The IRS has valuation standards you can apply to your gift giving. Basically, you can deduct the fair market value of noncash contributions to any qualified charitable organization. Refer to IRS Publication No. 78 for a list of qualified organizations.

Charitable Contributions can be a win, win, win proposition for all involved parties. The charity wins because it meets its goals. The donor wins because he or she gets a tax deduction, and may also satisfy philanthropic desires. The government wins by not having to provide the service provided by the charity.

Notes:

There is no practical limit on noncash charitable contributions to IRS approved charities that need donations.

You can also deduct car mileage at the rate of 14 cents a mile if you use your car for charitable purposes, plus parking fees and tolls.

The advantage of giving away appreciated property, such as a stock, is that you realize a write-off for the current market value of the gift, rather than what you originally paid for it, and you avoid having to pay tax on the profit that accumulated while you owned it. But, to get the maximum tax benefit from the contribution of appreciated property, make certain it qualifies as a long-term capital gain, which is property held for more than one year.

If you donate your used car to charity, you may be entitled to a charitable deduction equal to the fair market value of the car, according to the 'Blue Book'.

Consider making larger contributions in years in which you are subject to a higher marginal tax rate.

If you donate property that has decreased in value, below your original cost, it is better to first sell the property, realize the capital loss, and then donate the proceeds.

There are annual limitations on charitable deductions based on the type of contribution and the total of the taxpayers' Adjusted Gross Income.

CHARITABLE CONTRIBUTION JOURNAL

Date	Organization Name/Address	Property Description	Acquisition Date/Method	Fair Market Value	Actual Receipt

CASUALTY AND THEFT LOSSES...

A Casualty Loss is the damage, destruction or loss of property resulting from an identifiable event that is sudden, unexpected or unusual. Note: Special rules and limitations do apply.

Types of Supporting Evidence Include:
- Newspaper Clippings   _____
- Police Reports   _____
- Insurance Reports   _____
- Photographs   _____

Typical Types of Related Expenses:
- Appraisal Fees   _____
- Cleanup Costs   _____
- Repair Costs   _____
- Other   _____

List all lost, stolen, damaged, vandalized, confiscated or destroyed items:

Date of Loss	Date Acquired	Property Description	Cost or Basis	Fair Market Value Before	After	Serial #	Type of Loss	Amount Ins. Paid

LISTING OF COMMON ITEMIZED MISCELLANEOUS DEDUCTIONS...

Good tax planning starts with knowing about all of the allowable deductions that are available to you and your family. Most miscellaneous itemized deductions are deductible only to the extent that they exceed 2 percent of your Adjusted Gross Income. Certain miscellaneous deductions are subject to additional criteria and may be fully deductible or nondeductible.

Miscellaneous Deductions	Year Recap Amount
• Other Investment Expenses	_____
• Safe-deposit box fees to hold investments.	_____
• Continuing Education Expenses	_____
• Personal Living Expenses on a Temporary Job Assignment	_____
• All Job Hunting Expenses	_____
• Employment Agency Fees	_____
• Unreimbursed Employee Business Expenses	_____
• Business Gifts	_____
• Dues Paid to Professional or Service Organizations	_____
• Home Office Expenses	_____
• Income Producing Expenses	_____
• Indirect Deductions of Partnerships & S Corporations	_____
• Investment Advisory Fees	_____
• Investment Books & Computer Programs	_____
• Trustee's Administrative Fees	_____
• Legal Fees to produce taxable income	_____
• Legal Fees in collection of alimony	_____
• Court Costs (With Limitations)	_____
• Damages Paid for breach of contract or lease	_____
• Safe Deposit Box Rent	_____
• Professional Subscriptions	_____
• Tax Preparation Fees	_____
• Tax Consulting Fees	_____
• Gambling Losses to offset gambling winnings	_____
Subtotal:	_____

	Year Recap Amount
## Miscellaneous Deductions	
• Supplemental Unemployment Benefits	_____
• Self-employed Net Operating Loss Deductions	_____
• Business Casualty & Theft Losses	_____
• Business Related Travel Expenses	_____
• Business Related Entertainment Expenses	_____
• Business Car Lease Financing Costs	_____
• Business Car Depreciation	_____
• Business Car Standard Mileage Deduction	_____
• Business Loan Interest	_____
• Business Telephone	_____
• IRA/Keogh Fund Fees	_____
• Personal Property Taxes	_____
• Union Dues, Fees, Fines and Assessments	_____
• Uniforms	_____
• Cellular Telephones	_____
• Bad Debts	_____
• Uncollectible Loans	_____
• Custodial Fees	_____
• Appraisal fees for casualty losses	_____
• Appraisal fees for charitable contributions	_____
• Commute costs to second job.	_____
• Commute costs to job related class.	_____
• Employee contributions to a state disability fund.	_____
• Impairment related work expenses	_____
• Special equipment for the disabled.	_____
• Lead Paint Removal	_____
• Early Withdrawal of Savings Penalty	_____
• Business Tools with life of 1 year or less.	_____
• Embezzlement Losses	_____
• Protective Clothing required at work.	_____
• Personal Liability Insurance	_____

Totals: ═══════════

TRAVEL AND ENTERTAINMENT EXPENSES..

Travel and Entertainment expenses that are not employer reimbursed, but are directly related, and ordinary and necessary to your trade or business, and are income-producing activities, are usually deductible if you maintain adequate records, receipts and a diary.

The allowable deduction for Travel and Entertainment is limited to 50% of the amount spent, including taxes and tips. The tax rules define 'travel' as basically travel that requires overnight rest.

Notes: As of April 1, 1999 the standard mileage rate is 31 cents per mile for all miles of business use.
The standard daily meal expense rate or per diem rate, varies from $30 to $42 per day, depending upon the city involved.

Expense Type Codes:

• Transportation Fares	(TF)	• Automobile Expenses	(AA)
• Costs of Meals	(ME)	• Cost of Lodging	(LE)
• Baggage Charges	(BC)	• Telephone Charges	(TC)
• Cover Charges	(CC)	• Parking Fees	(PF)
•Ticket Face Value	(TV)	• Tips and Taxes	(TT)
• Laundry & Cleaning Exp.	(LC)	• Other Business Expenses	(OB)
• Gifts	(GT)	• Taxis	(TX)
• Auto Rental	(AR)		
_____	(_)	_____	(_)

TRAVEL/ENTERTAINMENT JOURNAL

Date	Time	Duration Business Discussion	Place/ Description/ Persons	Business Purpose/ Relationship	Expense Type Code	Amount

DETAILED AUTO EXPENSE TRACKING JOURNAL

Purpose Codes: B = Business   C = Charitable
                       I = Investment   M = Medical

Auto Expense Codes: G = Gas   O = Oil
                            T = Tolls   P = Parking
                            R = Repairs M = Miscellaneous

Date	Destination/ Contact	Purpose Code	Mileage Odometer Begin	End	Mileage	Auto Expenses Amount Code	Type

EDUCATIONAL EXPENSES...

In general, educational expenditures are deductible if the education:
- Maintains or improves skills required in your employment or business.
- Meets the express requirements of your employer as a condition of employment.

Examples Include:

	Year Recap Amount
• Tuition	_____
• Books	_____
• Supplies	_____
• Lab Fees	_____
• Travel Costs	_____
• Transportation Costs	_____
• Bar Examination Fee	_____
• Registration Fees	_____
• Away Meals and Lodging Expenses	_____
• Interest on Student Loans	_____

Notes:

All programs are subject to various eligibility and conditional criteria.

If you and your spouse together make $120,000 a year or more, make your children legally independent, so that they may qualify for the Hope Education Credit.

Educational Tax Programs Include:

A. The Hope Credit	_____
B. Lifetime Learning Credit	_____
C. Education IRA Withdrawals	_____
D. Traditional & Roth IRA Withdrawals	_____
E. Interest Paid on Student Loans	_____
F. Qualified State Tuition Programs	_____
G. Qualified U.S. Savings Bonds	_____
H. Employer's Educational Assistance Programs	_____

JOB HUNTING EXPENSES JOURNAL

You do not have to actually change jobs in order to deduct job hunting expenses. Job searching expenses are deductible as long as you are actively seeking a new job and it is doing the same type of work that you are presently doing.

Expenses Type Codes:

• Transportation Costs	(TC)	• Resume Printing	(RP)
• Postage	(PO)	• Phone Calls	(PC)
• Lodging	(LO)	• fi Meal Costs	(MC)
• Outplacement Agency	(OT)		
_____	(_)	_____	(_)

Date	Where	Why	Contact	Expense Type	Amount

ALIMONY/CHILD SUPPORT JOURNAL

Instruction: Circle Pd. or Rec'd.

Date Pd. / Rec'd.	Reference Child's Name	Amounts Alimony	Child Support

Notes:

CHAPTER V

TAX CREDITS AND TAX STRATEGIES

1. Examples of Various Tax Credits
2. Family Tax Planning Strategies
3. Other Tax Planning Strategies
4. Money Saving Investment Strategies
5. Income Reducing Strategies

EXAMPLES OF VARIOUS TAX CREDITS...

Take advantage of special tax credits that allow for a dollar-for-dollar offset to your final tax liability. **Note:** All credits have specific criteria and limitations that apply.

Examples Include:	Annual Costs/ Notes
• Dependent Care Credits (Form 2441)	_____
• Credits for the Elderly or Disabled (Schedule R)	_____
• Credit for Excess Social Security Withholding	_____
• Qualified Adoption Expense Credit(Form 8839)	_____
• The Hope Scholarship Credit (Form 8863)	_____
• Lifetime Learning Credit (Form 8863)	_____
• The Foreign Tax Credit (Form 1116)	_____
• The Earned Income Credit (Form EIC)	_____
• Real Estate Rehabilitation Tax Credit	_____
• Low-Income Housing Tax Credit	_____
• General Business Credit (Form 3800)	_____
• Credit for Excise Taxes paid on the Use of Gasoline & Special Fuels (Form 4136)	_____
• Child Tax Credit	_____
• Additional Child Tax Credit (Form 8812)	_____

Notes:

Child & Dependent Care Credit

You may qualify for the Dependent Care Credit, if you care for an individual who is your dependent, lives with you, and is under age 13, or physically and mentally cannot take care of himself or herself, and you must hire help in order for you or your spouse to seek employment or go to work.

Earned Income Credit

An employee whose income is below a certain threshold amount may be eligible to claim an Earned Income Credit. It is a special type of credit because it can exceed tax liability and is thus, also known as a refundable credit.

Credit for the Elderly and Permanently and Totally Disabled

If you or your spouse is 65 years old or older or you are permanently and totally disabled, you may be entitled to a credit of as much as $1,125 against your taxes.

Low-Income Housing Tax Credit

Invest in a publicly sold partnership that buys apartments and rents them to low-income people and receive tax credits equal to about 15 percent of your investment, each year for 10 years.

Real Estate Rehabilitation

A 10 percent tax credit is available on money spent to rehab buildings built before 1936, and historic rehabs qualify for a 20 percent tax credit.

General Business Credit

The investment credit has been combined with the alcohol fuel credit and the research credit into one general business credit.

Credit for Excise Taxes Paid

A credit or refund is available for the federal excise tax paid on gasoline for non highway business use, qualified business and taxicab use, commercial fishing vessel use, and certain aviation use.

Foreign Tax Credit

An individual may elect to claim a credit instead of a deduction for foreign income taxes.

Credit for Adoption Expenses

Qualified taxpayers who adopt a child are entitled to claim a maximum non-refundable credit of $5,000 per child.

Hope Scholarship Credit

Available for payment of any student's first two years of post secondary tuition and related expenses. The credit is 100% of the first $1,000 of expenses and 50% of the next $1,000.

Lifetime Learning Credit

Used for qualified tuition and expenses for courses to acquire or improve job skills, as well as for undergraduate and graduate level courses at an eligible educational institution. The credit is 20% of up to $5,000 of expenses to a maximum of $1,000 per return.

Adoption Credit

Refunds to the taxpayer the first $5,000 for expenses paid to adopt a qualifying child. An eligible child is generally under the age of 18 or one who is physically or mentally incapable of caring for themselves.

Mortgage Interest Credit

Issued by a state or local government via a Mortgage Credit Certificate (MCC). Amounts to a direct credit against your taxes. Must be obtained before you buy your home or get a mortgage.

FAMILY TAX PLANNING STRATEGIES...

Some of the ways families might use the tax laws to their advantage include the following:

Notes

- Choosing the most advantageous filing status. If you or your spouse is in a lower tax bracket or if one of you has large itemized deductions, filing separately may lower your total taxes. Filing separately may also lower the phase out of itemized deductions.

- You may be able to claim elderly parents who did not live with you if you provided more than 50 percent of their support.

- You may qualify for the tax advantages of 'head of household' or surviving spouse if you are single and have a child who lives with you.

- Even if you are married, check to determine if filing separate returns rather than a joint return is more beneficial.

- If you are blind or 65 years of age or older, you may be able to claim additional standard deductions.

- Plan to maximize the tax benefits of the personal exemption.

- Hire a child in your business, because your child can earn up to $4,000 during the year without having to pay or even file a federal income tax return.

- Children 14 or older can have as much as $25,350 in taxable income and pay tax in the 15 percent tax bracket.

- Children under age 14 can have up to $1,400 worth of taxable investment income without paying tax on it.

- In an effort to tax income at the lowest possible marginal tax rate, consider income splitting among family members, but be careful not to lose a dependency exemption through income shifting. Title bank accounts, securities, and other property in joint names.

- Time marriage or divorce to minimize the tax impact.
  Notes: Wait till next year to marry if both parties have a high income. When one spouse has little or no income, it is usually best to delay divorce until the next year.

- The payer of marital support should get a written agreement or court order in order to get the tax deduction for mandatory support payments.

- Get the custodial parent to execute Form 8332, so that you as a non-custodial parent can claim the children as dependents.

- Consider giving gifts to your children while you are alive, because they are in a lower tax bracket and will pay less taxes on the money.

- Baby-sitter and Day Care Center expenses for your child may be deductible if you know their name, address and social security number or the EIN number of their company.

- Consider gifting to a 'Generation-Skipping Dynasty Trust', which when established on behalf of your loved ones, can avoid estate and gift taxes for up to three generations.

- You may enjoy tax advantages by buying a house or condo, in full or in part, for your children to live in or renting to low-income elderly parents.

- Consider the tax benefits of taking a dependent exemption for your married child and having the child file as 'married filing separately'.

OTHER TAX SAVINGS STRATEGIES...

Notes

- You can deduct personal property taxes on such items as your car and boat, if they are:
  - Based only on the value of the property; and
  - Charged on an annual basis, even if collected more or less often than once a year.

- Many employee fringe benefits come to you tax-free and it may be advantageous to ask your employer to cut your salary, and to divert more of your pay to retirement benefits.

- Actively manage your marginal tax rate, which is affected by the filing status you select. It determines how much of any extra earnings you are able to keep and the savings power of deductible expenses.

- If you plan to work after your scheduled retirement date, consider how the income will affect your social security benefits.

- If you change jobs, leave the money in the company retirement plan or roll it over to an IRA, or other qualified plan.

MONEY SAVING INVESTMENT STRATEGIES

Your Investment Strategy should strive for a combination of compounding the principal amount without making tax payments, and realizing a lower tax rate at the point of withdrawal, which probably means in your retirement years or for a government approved reason. Generally, it is better to defer gains to a later year, and to accelerate losses so that you have the use of the money for a longer period of time. But, inflation or function may necessitate spending now.

Always consider the impact of your Capital Gains on your Adjusted Gross Income (AGI), because your AGI will determine if certain itemized deductions will not be allowed or if your personal exemptions are decreased.

Notes

- Adjust your W-4 to stop the withdrawal of excess withholding taxes, and put the money into a tax-deferred Individual Retirement Account or a 401(K) plan. _____ _____ _____

- Participate in Employee Retirement Plans, as a tax-cutting strategy, because you are not taxed on the earnings in your retirement account until you begin withdrawing the funds. _____ _____ _____ _____

- Use stock losses to help offset the gains on other investments, and to lower your overall tax bill. (Special Section 1244 Stock) _____ _____ _____

- Engage in profit-taking, because only $3,000 of net losses a year can be used to offset income, other than capital gains, with the tax value of extra capital losses postponed to future years. _____ _____ _____ _____

- Do not take a lump sum distribution from your pension plan, unless you roll it over into an IRA account in a timely way. _____ _____

- Invest in Series EE Savings Bonds, because the interest income is not recognized until it is received, which is when the bonds are redeemed. _____ _____ _____

- The interest from Series EE Bonds may be exempt from federal tax, if their redemption proceeds are used for certain educational needs.

- When the Series EE Bonds come due, exchange them for Series HH Bonds, so that you can avoid recognizing the Series EE Bond interest until the Series HH Bonds are redeemed.

- Consider a Roth IRA, which provides for tax-exempt withdrawals under certain circumstances.

- If you own publicly traded stock that will produce a long-term capital gain when sold, use the gain to make a charitable contribution.

- Always consider the after-tax yield of an investment, when comparing the expected returns from various types of investments.

- Consider Deferred Annuities for retirement savings, because they do not have taxes on earnings taken out annually, which means the tax money continues to earn interest for you.

- Establish a Charitable Remainder Trust (CRT), because by gifting to the CRT, you may avoid capital gains tax on the appreciated assets held by the trust.

- Setup a Family Limited Partnership to shift investment income to family members in lower income brackets.

- Consider selling passive assets to free up some of your large passive loss carryovers.

- If you purchased at original issuance, on or after August 1, 1993, any shares of qualified small business stock, and you realize a capital gain after holding the stock for more than 5 years, you may exclude 50% of the gain when the shares are sold or exchanged.

- Within limits, you can elect to rollover any capital gain _____ if you purchase other small business stock during the _____ 60 day period beginning on the sale date. _____

- Limited Partnerships can pay distributions that are _____ partially sheltered from income tax. _____

- Consider selling stock or mutual fund shares before the _____ ex-dividend date because this can produce long-term _____ capital gains as opposed to dividends payments which _____ serve to reduce the asset price and are taxed as _____ ordinary income. _____

- Tax-Swap securities to accelerate losses without _____ significantly changing your overall investment position. _____

- Exchange business or investment property for like-kind _____ property without incurring tax on your gain. _____

- Report your gain under the limitations of the installment _____ sale method, if payments are to be received in more _____ than one year. _____

INCOME REDUCING STRATEGIES...

Generally, it is to your advantage to defer receiving income to a later year. And, it is the date of actual receipt that determines the year in which the income is taxable.

Notes

- Create a deferred, written compensation agreement with your employer, and pay tax on the deferred income only when it is received.
  - Take income when you expect to be in a lower tax bracket.
  - Take income when it will even out your income stream.

- Use the 401(k) plan offered by your employer to postpone income by deferring a certain portion of your salary on a pretax basis.

- If you qualify, consider using the 10 year averaging method on the long-term capital gain portion of a lump sum distribution rather than have it taxed as a long-term capital gain.

- Try to defer income if you expect income tax rates to be lowered in subsequent years.

- Switch salary from taxable compensation to nontaxable types of fringe benefit compensation.
  Examples include: Increased medical insurance, group life insurance, employer educational assistance.

- Consider joining a company Cafeteria Plan, where you reduce your salary by a given amount each year, to be used tax free for uninsured medical expenses, insurance or dependent care.

- Reduce your gross income by participating in dependent care assistance programs or qualified retirement plans.

- If your 'provisional income' falls within certain constraints, you can avoid paying federal income taxes on up to 85% of your social security benefits.

- Ask your employer to defer paying your year-end bonus until next year.

- Invest excess cash in Treasury Bills that mature next year.

- Rollover qualifying distributions from your employer's retirement plan to an IRA.

CHAPTER VI

ANTICIPATING AUDIT MATTERS

1. Substantiate All Information In Your Return
2. Checklist of Precautionary Measures
3. Know Your Taxpayer Rights

SUBSTANTIATE ALL INFORMATION IN YOUR RETURN

There are many steps that you can take to help audit-proof your tax return. Primarily, audit-proofing involves attaching to your return, the key information relevant to a specific deduction in your return. You should provide the information for deductions you think may raise a red flag by the IRS.

Typically, these red-flag deductions are of the following types:
- Charitable Contributions
- Mileage Claims
- Entertainment Costs
- The Home Office Deduction
- Unusual Medical Expenses

By including proof for suspected red-flag deductions with your return, you greatly reduce the need for an audit. Additionally, the IRS would rather not audit those taxpayers who are well-informed and prepared to intelligently respond to their audit challenge.

Proof may include any or all of the following:
- Copies of Canceled Checks
- Copies of Receipts
- An Affidavit

Additionally, returns with the following characteristics are more likely to be audited:
- Taxpayers who involve family members in their financial operations.
- If you prepare a complex return yourself.
- Use the services of a preparer who appears on the IRS's problem preparer list by way of reputation.
- Occupations which typically generate unreported cash income such as taxi-drivers and waiters, and self-employed contractors.
- Higher income taxpayers.
- Returns with passive income and losses.

Note: There is no reason to fear an audit when you have made an honest effort to comply with the IRS record keeping requirements.

For federal tax purposes, hold on to your records for at least three years from the date you file your return. After that point, the IRS can no longer call on you to prove your income or deductions, unless it suspects you have underreported your gross income by more than 25 percent. In that case, the IRS has 6 years to challenge your returns. If you fail to file altogether or file a fraudulent return, the IRS has an indefinite time limit to challenge your return. Additionally, some state statutes sometimes exceed federal limitations, so state returns should be kept for as long as 4 years after you file, depending on where you live.

AUDIT PRECAUTIONARY MEASURES:

The following measures are offered as a possible means of helping to avoid qualifying for an IRS audit.

CHECK

- Do not round off, unless specified by the IRS instructions. _____
- Use Form 8283, if you give items worth more than $500 to charity. ____
- Attach all required supporting schedules and forms to your return. _____
- Stop huge refunds by adjusting your withholding tax deductions. _____
- File on time and adhere to extension guidelines. _____
- Report all W-2 and 1099 income. _____
- Include the Social Security Numbers of all dependents. _____
- Be very careful when claiming dependents other than children, grandchildren and parents. _____
- Write or type neatly and legibly. _____
- Report the name, address, and identification numbers of all child care providers. _____
- Include Form 8275, which is called the Disclosure Statement, and use it to explain the specific grounds on which a deduction was taken. _____
- For all nontaxable income you receive, make a copy of the check you received, and put it in a handy yearly file with an explanation. _____
- Keep itemized deductions under 35% of your adjusted gross income. _____
- Avoid unreasonable positions, especially those that make you appear to not have a profit-making intent. _____
- Group your business expenses under the appropriate deductible headings, and avoid listing too much under 'Miscellaneous'. _____
- Keep travel, meals and entertainment expenses proportionate to your income. _____
- Thoroughly document your office-in-home deduction. _____
- Thoroughly document excessively high medical expenses. _____
- Thoroughly document all bad debt losses. _____
- Thoroughly document all casualty losses with police and insurance reports. _____
- Keep your depreciation calculations accurate. _____
- Be sure to include tip income when working for a business that typically receives gratuities. _____
- Be able to justify the high percentage of business use of your vehicle and the need for it in your occupation. _____

Procedural Guidelines:

Keep all of your receipts organized by using envelopes that are labeled with various types of deductions and expenses, and cross-reference those receipts to your entries in this guidebook.

KNOW YOUR TAXPAYER RIGHTS

As a taxpayer you have the following rights when engaged in an IRS audit.

1. You have the right to appeal any IRS decision on your tax liability and their collection actions.

2. You do not have to pay more than the correct amount of tax due under the law.

3. You can force the IRS to waive penalties, if you can demonstrate that you acted reasonably and in good faith, or relied upon the wrong advice of an IRS employee.

4. You have the right to make sound recordings of any meeting with the IRS, provided you inform them in writing 10 days prior to the meeting.

5. You have the right to be represented by an authorized party during the IRS audit.

6. You have the right to represent yourself before the IRS.

7. You have the right to demand professional, respectful treatment from IRS personnel.

8. You have the enforceable right to know what the IRS will do if you do not provide them with the requested information.

9. You have the right to know why the IRS is requesting certain information, and how the IRS intends to use that information.

10. You have the right to have the IRS safeguard your information privacy and confidentiality.

11. You have the right to have IRS agents spell out and protect your rights as a taxpayer throughout your contact with the agency

12. You have the right to read IRS Publication 1, which explains the Taxpayer's Bill of Rights, prior to your audit.

13. You can appeal an Audit or Examination Report by sending a protest letter to the local IRS District Director within 30 days of receipt of the report, and requesting a meeting with an Appeal Officer.

14. If your appeal fails, you still have the right to file a petition in Tax Court with the help of a tax attorney.

15. You have the right to make a Freedom of Information Act request for the auditor's records.

16. IRS field auditors cannot enter your home without a court order or your permission.

17. If you are missing receipts or other documents, you have the right to reconstruct those records.

18. You have the right to speak to the auditor's manager if you think the auditor is treating you unfairly.

19. You have the right to negotiate tax issues in an appeal.

20. If the audit is not going well, you have the right to demand a recess in order to consult a tax professional or to get your records in order.

21. You have the right to have the IRS complete the audit within three years of the date the tax return is filed, unless the IRS finds tax fraud or a significant underreporting of income.

22. You have the right to supply the auditor with no more information than he or she is entitled to.

23. You have the right to protest an IRS seizure or the threat of a seizure by filing Form 911, Application for Taxpayer Assistance Order, Form 9423, Collection Appeal or Form 12153, Application for Collection Due Process Hearing.

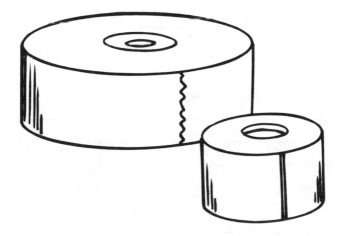

Notes:

CHAPTER VII

FREQUENTLY ASKED QUESTIONS

THE MOST FREQUENTLY ASKED QUESTIONS

Should I open an Education IRA?

Yes. The Education IRA was created to give a tax break to families trying to save for children's college education. Beginning in 1998, you can make yearly contributions to this special type of IRA. The most you can contribute, per year, is $500 per beneficiary under 18 years old. When you later withdraw the money from the IRA to pay for qualified higher education expenses, the withdrawals will generally be tax-free. The contributions are not deductible. Note: Be sure no one else has an education IRA for the same child.

What other types of credits are available for post secondary school education and job retraining?

Under the Taxpayer Relief Act of 1997, individual taxpayers are allowed an income tax credit for an amount equal to the Hope Scholarship Credit and the Lifetime Learning Credit as follows:
* Hope Scholarship Credit equals up to $1,500 per year per student, if in their freshman or sophomore years of undergraduate school for specific expenses.
* Lifetime Learning Credit equals up to $1,000 per student through 2002, then $2,000, for anyone who qualifies.

Note: Both credits are subject to income phase out limits.

How does a Roth IRA differ from a regular IRA?

The Roth IRA is a 'nondeductible' IRA. The taxpayer contributes to it with funds that have already been taxed, instead of deferring the tax on that money until the funds are withdrawn from the IRA later. With a regular IRA, your earnings are always taxed later, but with a Roth IRA, they are never taxed. Generally, if you leave your funds in the Roth IRA for the requisite five years from when the first year contributions are made, and you withdraw funds for an allowed purpose, such as a first time home purchase or die or become age 59fi, then your distributions are tax-free. Additionally, the Roth IRA is not subject to the minimum distribution rules when the taxpayer turns age 70fi, and contributions can be made to a Roth IRA even after the taxpayer turns 70fi.

What is the maximum amount that joint filers can contribute to IRAs?

The amount that joint filers can contribute to IRAs in one year can total as much as $4,000. Joint filers can contribute as much as $2,000 for each spouse, provided the combined earned income of both spouses is at least equal to the contributed amount.

Is any of the money I pay for daycare tax deductible?

Yes. You may be able to deduct 20 to 30% of your daycare expenses directly from your tax bill, as long as your expenses are to enable you to work or look for work.

My mom lives with us. Can we claim her as a dependent?

Yes. Your mother can be your dependent if she meets all five of the standard dependency tests, but she cannot claim her own personal exemption on her own return. Importantly, your mother must have less than $2,700 of gross income subject to tax, and you must contribute more than 50% toward her total support.

How can I avoid the mandatory withholding of 20% on distributions eligible for rollover to an IRA?

Make sure the plan transfers the funds directly to the IRA through a trustee-to-trustee payment.

How much is the Child Tax Credit and who qualifies?

In 1999, the Child Tax Credit is $500 per child. The child must be under the age of 17, be a US citizen, national or resident of the US, have a taxpayer identification number, and be one of the following for a full year, except in the case of death:
- A son or daughter.
- A descendent of a son or daughter
- A step son of step daughter
- An eligible foster child.

What can I do to save taxes if I fall short of being able to itemize deductions each year by a few hundred dollars?

Consider bunching deductions into alternating years so that you can itemize every two years and claim the standard deduction in the other years.

My mother-in-law cares for our children while we go to work. We pay her $200 per week. Do we qualify for the dependent care credit?

Yes. You get the credit as long as you and your wife do not claim your mother-in-law as a dependent. If your mother-in-law comes to your home to daycare, you are required to pay social security and unemployment taxes based on her salary. But, if you take your children to her home, you will not have these payroll responsibilities. In any event, your mother-in-law is subject to income and self-employment tax on this income.

My son and his wife want to purchase a home, but they cannot raise the down payment. What is the best way for me to help them make the purchase?

Consider entering a shared equity arrangement with them. Your son and his wife will then pay you for the fair rental value of your fractional share of ownership, and you will be able to offset the income with mortgage interest, property taxes, related expenses and your percentage share of the depreciation expense.

I just bought a new car and would like to donate my old car to the local high school. Can I get a tax break for giving the car to the school and at what value?

Yes, you can claim the car's present market value as a charitable contribution. But, you must get a written statement of the car's value from either a used car dealer or the 'Blue Book', and a written receipt that describes the car from the school.

Can I take a deduction for the weight loss program I am on?

Yes, but only if the weight loss program has been prescribed by your doctor in order to treat a specific ailment.

What types of interest payments are not deductible?

Personal interest, such as interest on credit cards, car loans, and tax deficiencies is not deductible. Restructure your debt using home equity loans.

Can you use real estate losses to offset wages, interest, dividends, and gains from stock market investments?

No. Real Estate losses, which are considered to be passive losses, can only be used to offset passive income, in most situations. The gain from the sale of real estate can only be offset by other capital losses and passive losses. Note: Refer to Chapter III for further information.

I am thinking about starting a home-based business. What form of business organization should I choose?

It might be smart to delay incorporating for a year or two, or to initially elect 'S' corporation status, or form an LLC and then convert it to a corporation, so that you can take maximum advantage of startup losses on your personal income tax return. **Note:** Talk to an attorney or CPA.

I went through a divorce last year and paid a lot of legal fees. Are these fees deductible?

Legal fees for divorce itself and for property settlement are not deductible, but legal fees to collect taxable income, such as alimony are deductible as miscellaneous itemized deductions, subject to the 2 percent limit.

I refinanced my home last year and paid points. Are they deductible?

Points paid solely to refinance your home mortgage cannot be entirely deducted in the year paid. They must be deducted over the life of the loan.

When should I consider 'itemizing'?

Complete your list of itemized deductions and compare the total with your standard deduction. Then choose the larger of the two deduction amounts.

How can I qualify for the earned income credit?

You may take this credit if a child did not live with you and you earned less than $10,030 or if a child lived with you and you earned less than $26,473. **Note:** Other rules do apply.

I do a lot of volunteer work. Can I deduct the value of my time?

No. You cannot deduct the value of volunteer services.

Are my credit card finance charges deductible?

Only, if you use your credit card to make purchases for your business. If you also make use of the card for non-business expenses, only the finance charges attributable to business purchases can be deducted.

I recently sold some antiques and works of art. What tax rates apply?

Collectibles are taxed at higher rates than gains from selling other types of capital assets, which have been held longer than one year. Instead of a 20% top rate, a collectibles gain is taxed at a maximum 28% rate.

How are Social Security benefits taxed under the federal personal income tax?

Social Security benefits are not subject to federal personal income tax if the taxpayer's provisional income is below the base amount of $32,000 for Married Filing Joint filers, and $25,000 for all others.

How will my divorce affect my taxes?

You cannot file jointly if you are now legally divorced or separated. If you have children, the spouse that has custody of the child for most of the year is the one entitled to claim that child as a dependent. If you receive alimony, you must include it as a taxable income. If you are paying out alimony, you can deduct these payments from your taxable income.

How does working affect the Social Security benefits I receive?

If you are between the ages of 62 and 65, you lose out on $1.00 of Social Security benefits for every $2.00 you earn above $9,120 for 1999. Unearned income does not penalize your benefits. Between the ages of 65 and 68, you lose $1.00 of Social Security benefits for every $3.00 earned above $14,500 in 1999.

What do I do if I cannot pay my taxes?

File your tax return on time, and attach to the front either a completed Form 9465, Installment Agreement Request, or your own written request for a payment plan, stating the amount and the date you can pay each month. Also, pay as much as you can with the return. Or, call the IRS to establish an installment agreement, as soon as you become aware of your tax liability.

Do I have to pay tax on reinvested dividends?

Yes. If you receive more shares of stock instead of cash dividends, you must report the dividends as income at a stock price equal to its fair market value. Other rules may also apply.

Is severance pay taxable?

Yes. Amounts you receive as severance pay are taxable as income in the year you receive them.

Can I get rid of my past tax liability in bankruptcy?

You can discharge income taxes in bankruptcy under certain circumstances, but you need to speak to a competent bankruptcy attorney for specific advice on your case.

What is meant by the term, 'offer-in-compromise'?

The IRS allows taxpayers who cannot pay their back taxes to submit an 'offer' for the amount owed, plus the promise to timely file all tax returns and pay all taxes for the next 5 years.

How do I get a copy of a prior tax return?

Use Form 4506 to request copies of previously filed and processed tax returns or Form W-2 only. There is a charge of $23.00 for each tax period requested. Tax return transcripts and copies of Forms W-2 only will be provided at no charge.

My income this year is larger than last year's. Can I average my income for the last two years? (Income

averaging is only available to farmers)

No. Income averaging is no longer available. You can only delay income from one year to the next.

Questions You Want To Ask Your Tax Preparer/Advisor:

Question:

_____

_____

_____

Response:

_____

_____

_____

Question:

_____

_____

_____

Response:

_____

_____

_____

Question:

_____

_____

_____

Response:

_____

_____

_____

CHAPTER VIII

APPENDIX

1. Financial Calendar for Individuals

2. Glossary of Terms

3. Useful Reference Resources

4. Recommended Other Service Providers

5. National Taxpayer and Research Organizations

6. Develop A Three-Year Plan

7. Important Phone Numbers and Addresses

8. Notes

THE FINANCIAL CALENDAR FOR INDIVIDUALS

Due Date	Status	Form	Date Paid	Amt.
January 15	___	Estimated Payment (Form 1040-ES) Declaration of Estimated Tax for fourth quarter of prior year.	___	___
February 1	___	W-2s are due from your employer.	___	___
April 15	___	Form 1040 Individual income tax return, including employment taxes for household employees, for prior year	___	___
		Form 4868 Request for automatic four-month extension.	___	___
		Form 709 or 709A Gift tax return for prior year	___	___
		Estimated Payment (Form 1040-ES For first quarter of current yr.)	___	___
June 15	___	Estimated Payment (Form 1040-ES for second quarter).	___	___
July	___	Midyear Planning Review	___	___
August 15	___	Form 1040 for prior year Form 2688 for further two-month extension.	___	___
		Form 709 or 709A, if previously extended by Form 4868.	___	___
September 15	___	Estimated Payment (Form 1040-ES for third quarter).	___	___
October 15	___	Form 1040 for prior year (If previous extensions filed).	___	___
December 31	___	Last day for charitable and education IRA contributions to be eligible for the current year tax return inclusion.	___	___

Special Events To Contact A Professional Advisor

- Inheritance
- Death
- Adoption
- Birth
- Catastrophic Loss
- Involuntary Conversion
- Estate Planning
- Retirement Planning
- Financial Physical
- Taxability of Fringe Benefits

GLOSSARY OF TERMS

Active Income

Income derived from a business entity in which the owner or shareholder materially and regularly participates in the business operations.

Affidavit

Oral testimony presented in the form of a written statement. A detailed letter of explanation, that is notarized and includes a declaration that the statements are made under penalty of perjury. It can substitute for receipts or canceled checks, in the event other records are not available.

Accelerated Deductions

The practice of paying deductible expenses in late December, rather than paying them in the following year.

Active Participation Test

Requires that the investor makes final decisions with respect to the investment and the taxpayer must devote a minimum amount of time to the activity. Must meet this test to deduct up to $25,000 of losses from rental real estate.

Adjusted Gross Income (AGI)

Calculated by subtracting the basic tax adjustments or expenses from your gross income. To qualify for many other tax deductions, eligibility is determined by the level of AGI.

Alternative Minimum Tax (AMT)

An additional tax equal to the tentative minimum tax less the regular income tax liability. AMT is intended to charge certain taxpayers a minimum tax in the event they have incomes which have been sheltered to a great extent, such that they would otherwise pay far less than what is considered 'fair'. The AMT rates presently climb to a maximum of 28% for alternative minimum taxable income in excess of $175,000.

Amended Return

A revised tax return, filed with Form 1040X to correct an error on a prior return filed within the previous three years.

Amount Realized

Equal to Net Sale or the sale price minus commissions, fees and any other costs of the sale.

'At Risk'

In most cases, an investor may not deduct losses in excess of the amount for which the investor is at risk. Amounts at risk include any amounts of cash invested, any amounts financed which have personal liability, and qualified nonrecourse financing.

Average Tax Rate

Taxes as a fraction of income. Total Taxes divided by Total Taxable Income.

Back-End Fees

Also known as Redemption Fees. Fees deducted from your fund when you redeem or sell shares.

Basis

The purchase price of your home, plus your costs of acquisition, and improvement costs. Used to calculate your taxable gain after selling the property. The basis of investment property is the purchase price minus accumulated depreciation.

Bubble Brackets

These are hidden income tax rate increases used by the government to take away certain benefits from taxpayers whose incomes fall within various income ranges. At certain specific income
levels, each extra dollar of extra income add more than one dollar to the amount the IRS gets to tax. It has the negative effect of raising your effective marginal rate.

Bunching

Used by taxpayers on the itemize-or-not borderline. The practice of timing expenses to produce lean and fat years. In alternating years, you load in as many deductible expenses as possible to exceed the standard deduction amount and qualify for a larger write-off.

Burned-Out Shelter

A shelter that produced tax write-offs in its early years, but the investment is now producing taxable income.

Cafeteria Plan

Also known as a Flexible Benefit Plan. Permits the employee to select between taxable and nontaxable benefits which are excludable from your income.

Community Trust

A public charity in which you may establish a separate account.

Cost Basis

The starting point for figuring a gain or loss if you later sell your home or for figuring depreciation if you later use part of your home for business purposes or for rent.

Capital Gain Income

Realized by individuals on dispositions of qualifying assets. These assets are generally taxed at lower rates than ordinary income.

Capital Improvements

An improvement that materially adds to the value of your home, considerably prolongs its useful life or adopts it to new uses. You must add the cost of any improvements to the basis of your home. You cannot deduct these costs on your personal residence. Improvements for business or rental properties must be capitalized and depreciated. Examples include adding a bathroom, finishing your basement and installing a new roof.

Deferred Annuities

You give money to some other party, usually an insurance company, for the long-term. Your account builds up because you promise not to withdraw funds for many years, and there is no current income tax until you withdraw your money. Research the negative aspects of the annuity.

Deferred Compensation Arrangement

An employer's unfunded promise to pay the employee at a later date, in order to delay income tax liability.

Deferred Giving (Gifting)

Involves a present gift to charity of the future use of a property. The advantage is you get an income deduction now.

Deminimis Fringe Benefits

Those of little value and are not taxed to employees. Examples include occasional personal use of business telephones and copiers.

Dependent Care Credit

You may be eligible if you incur expenses to care for your child so that you, or, if married, you and your spouse are able to go to work.

Depreciation

The process of deducting a portion of the cost of an asset on a yearly basis due to loss of value as it wears or becomes obsolescent.

Discriminate Function System (DIF)

An IRS software program used to select returns to be audited. Compares deductions, credits and exemptions with the norms for taxpayers in each income bracket.

Earned Income

Compensation for your personal services. Includes salary, commissions, and tips.

Enrolled Agent

A tax preparer who passes an IRS test and experience requirements, and can represent clients at IRS audits and appeals.

Estimated Tax

If you have income not subject to withholding, you may have to make quarterly payments of the estimated amount needed to cover your expected tax liability for the year. You can be penalized if estimated payments are not within $1,000 of 90% of the tax owed.

Excludable Income

Income treated as an exclusion and is not included in your gross income as taxable income.

Fair Market Value

The price at which property would change hands between a willing buyer and seller, with both parties having reasonable informed knowledge of all the pertinent facts.

Fiduciary

A person who holds assets in trust for a beneficiary.

Flexible Spending Account (FSA)

Also known as a Reimbursement Account or Salary Reduction Plan. Used to lower employee income and FICA taxes, and save the employer payroll tax costs. Employees are able to pay health insurance premiums, and unreimbursed medical expenses or dependent care expenses through a pretax salary reduction.

401(K) Plans

A plan which may be offered by your employer, in which you may elect to defer a certain amount of your salary on a before-tax basis. These amounts are withheld from your salary and are not reported as income until withdrawn from the plan. Income earned on your 401(K) investment is tax-deferred, and unlike an IRA, you may be able to borrow from the plan without penalty.

Front-End Fees

Also known as Purchase Fees or Load Charges. They reduce your investment in mutual funds, but are considered part of your cost basis for tax purposes.

General Partnerships

The investor is a general partner with a working interest, and there is no requirement for material participation to claim tax deductions, but the investor is individually liable for the partnership's debts, even if they exceed the amount of investment.

Gift Tax

You may give up to $10,000 yearly to as many people you want without being concerned about this tax. If it is owed, it is owed by the giver.

Home Equity

The current fair market value of a house, minus outstanding debt secured by the house.

Home Equity Debt

Any debt secured by a qualified residence that does not exceed the home's value.

Home Repairs

A repair keeps your home in an ordinary, efficient operating condition. It does not add to the value of your home or prolong its life. You cannot deduct repair costs and generally cannot add them to the basis of your home. Examples include repainting your house or replacing a broken window glass.

Individual Retirement Arrangements (IRAs)

A personal savings plan that lets you set aside funds for your retirement, using pretax dollars. Subject to some limitations, the amount you contribute to your IRA can be deducted from your taxable income, and earnings are not taxable until they are distributed to you.

Installment Sale

The sale of an asset in exchange for a specified series of payments.

Itemized Deductions

Write-offs for certain medical expenses, taxes, interest, charitable contributions, casualty and theft losses, as well as job expenses, and other miscellaneous itemized deductions.

Keogh Plan

A type of retirement plan available to the self-employed, and those who own their own business. You must have earned income from the trade or business for which the plan was created, in order to take a deduction for a contribution to the plan.

Kiddie Tax

A child under the age of 14 will be taxed on unearned income, such as interest and dividends, in excess of $1,400, at their parent's top marginal tax rate.

Life Estate Interest

An interest in property that terminates upon the death of the life estate's owner.

Like-kind Exchanges

Used to avoid paying taxes on appreciated business or investment property. Allows the taxpayer to reinvest profits without paying tax on them, under certain conditions. Applies only to real estate.

Limited Liability Company (LLC)

Offers real property owners limited liability protection from creditors in the event of a lawsuit, without the penalties of double taxation by incorporating, and partnership tax treatment benefits.

Long-Term Capital Gains

Gains on the sale of property held for more than 12 months are subject to a maximum 20% tax rate. Effective January 1, 2001 the maximum capital gains rate for assets that are held more than 5 years is 18 percent.

Marginal Tax Rate

The rate of tax you pay on your next dollar of taxable income.

Marriage Tax Penalty

Married partners who earn about the same income may pay more tax if they file a joint return or file separate married returns, than they would if they could file two single returns.

Medical Savings Account (MSA)

Contributions to this account, within limits, are tax deductible, and distributions are only includable in your income if not used to pay for medical expenses.

The Nanny Tax

Household employers can now pay social security, federal unemployment, and withheld federal income taxes through their individual income tax return, and are no longer required to file federal quarterly payroll returns.

Net Capital Loss

The excess of capital losses over capital gains. These losses can be deducted up to $3,000 per year. Larger losses must be carried forward to future years.

Passive Activity Income

The conduct of any trade or business in which the taxpayer does not materially participate on a regular, continuous and substantial basis. Losses from passive business involvements can only be used to offset passive income sources.

Personal Property

Any tangible property not permanently affixed to real property.

Phantom Income

Gains realized by a tax shelter investment to be taxed to respective investors without moneys to pay the related tax.

Points

A home buyer can deduct loan fees or points in the year of payment when the financing agreement provides that these fees are to be paid for the use of the lender's money. Points paid for the refinancing of a home loan are not currently deductible, and must be deducted over the life of the loan.

Premature Distributions

Withdrawals from a company retirement plan that are subject to a 10% penalty if you are under age 55 (in the year you leave your job), or under age 59fi (if you are still employed).

Prerefunded Bond

A municipal bond that is backed by Treasury Bonds.

Private Annuity

A person's promise to pay a fixed amount to another, called the annuitant, for life in return for the annuitant's transfer of property or cash to the person paying the annuity.

Private Foundation

An entity that you can establish to control your charitable activities. It must first qualify for tax-exempt status in order to make your charitable contributions tax deductible.

Provisional Income

Calculated by taking Adjusted Gross Income (without Social Security Benefits), plus tax-exempt interest, plus half of the Social Security Benefits.

Qualified Plan

An employee benefit plan that meets IRS requirements.

Rabbi Trust

An irrevocable trust established by the employer to pay deferred compensation to the employee. But, the employee is not protected if the employer becomes insolvent or goes into bankruptcy.

Real Estate Investment Trust (REIT)

A trust fund that holds a portfolio of real estate investments.

Remainder Interest

The donor retains an interest only for his or her lifetime in a personal residence or a farm.

Reverse Mortgage

Provides a source of income, and helps to reduce taxes by removing a large asset from your estate.

Rollover

A tax-free transfer of cash or other assets from a qualified retirement plan to an eligible retirement plan. Also, a loan renewal.

Roth IRA

Contributions to a Roth IRA are not deductible from your income tax, but qualified distributions are not includible in your taxable income. Primarily designed to help first-time homebuyers.

Second Home

A vacation home is considered a second home if it is used for personal purposes more than 14 days or 10% of the days rented, whichever is greater. The interest and real estate taxes remain deductible on a second home, without passive loss limitations.

Secular Trust

Funds held in a secular trust as part of a deferred compensation plan are not accessible by an employer's creditors. But, you must pay tax currently on any amounts contributed to the trust.

Short-Term Capital Gains

Gains on capital assets held for 12 months or less are treated as short term capital gains.

Simplified Employee Plan (SEP)

A retirement plan in which both employee and employer contribute to an IRA. Employees are vested immediately and pay no tax on the employer's contributions.

Standard Deduction

A set dollar amount deduction that varies with your elected filing status.

Stock Options

Allows an employee to buy a specified amount of stock from their employer at some set price and for a stated period of time. The employee only exercises his or her option if the stock price rises above the set exercise price, otherwise they let the option expire.

Tax Deferral Option

A feature of the IRS Code that capital gains tax on an asset is payable only when the gain is realized by selling the asset.

Tax Deferred Retirement Plan

Plans that allow contributions and earnings to be made and accumulate tax-free until they are paid out as benefits.

Tax-exempt Interest

Interest paid on bonds issued by states or municipalities that is tax-free for federal income tax purposes.

Tax Preferences

Specific deductions and credits which have been singled out by the tax code because they provide tax shelters. They range from a portion of depreciation expense to passive farm losses.

Tax Swap

The selling of securities at a loss for tax purposes and the replacing of them with the same or similar securities.

Taxable Income

Deduct your itemized deductions or the standard deduction, and any personal exemptions from your adjusted gross income.

Unearned Income

Income from investments. Includes interest, dividends and capital gains.

Wage Base

The level of earnings to which the full Social Security tax applies. For 2000 the full 15.3% tax applies to the first 76,200 of wages or self-employment income.

'Wash Sale' Rules

If you sell securities at a loss and purchase the same securities within 30 days before or after the sale, your loss is disallowed.

Zero-Coupon Bond

A bond that pays no interest until maturity.

USEFUL REFERENCE RESOURCES

- **IRS Online Forms and Instruction Access**
  www.irs.ustreas.gov/plain/forms_pubs/forms.html
  www.irs.ustreas.gov/prod/forms
  P 800-829-3676   P 800-829-1040

- **IRS Commissioner**
  1111 Constitution Ave., NW, 3000 IR, Washington, DC 20224
  P 202-622-4114

- **IRS Phone Directory**
  TimeValue Software, 4 Jenner Street, irvine CA 92618
  P 800-426-4741   F 949-727-3268
  www.timevalue.com/irsindex.html

- **Taxpayer Problem Resolution Program (PRP)/**
  Office of the Taxpayer Advocate
  Provides assistance to taxpayers whose problems are not resolved through-
  normal IRS channels.
  P 800-829-1040   P 877-777-4778

- **Plain Language Position of Proposed Regulations**
  www.irs.ustreas.gov/prod/tax_regs/reglist.html

- **American Institute of Certified Public Accountants**
  1211 Avenue of the Americas, New York, NY 10036-8775
  P 212-596-6200   F 212-596-6213   www.aicpa.org

- **American Accounting Association**
  5717 Bessie Drive, Sarasota, FL 34233
  P 941-921-7747   F 941-923-4093   E-mail: aaahq@packet.net

- **National Association of Tax Practitioners (NATP)**
  720 Association Drive, Appleton, WI 54914
  P 800-558-3402   F 920-749-1062   www.natptax.com
  Includes a state tax directory.

- **American Institute of Professional Bookkeepers**
  6001 Montrose Road, Suite 207, Rockville, MD 20852
  P 800-541-0066   www.aipb.org

- **The American Law Institute**
  4025 Chestnut Street, Philadelphia, PA 19104
  P 215-243-1600   F 215-243-1664   www.ali.org

- **Pennsylvania Institute of Certified Public Accountants**
  1608 Walnut Street, Philadelphia, PA 19103-5457
  P 215-735-2635   F 215-735-3694   www.picpa.com

- **National Society of Accountants**
  1010 N. Fairfax Street, Alexandria, VA 22314
  P 703-549-6400   F 703-549-2984   www.nsacct.org

- **American Association of Hispanic Certified Public Accountants**
  100 N. Main Street, PMB 406, San Antonio, TX 78205
  P 203-255-7003   F 203-259-2872   www.aahcpa.org

- **National Association of Enrolled Agents**
  200 Orchard Ridge Drive, Gaithersburg, MD 20878
  P 301-212-9608   F 301-990-1611   www.naea.org

- **American Society of Women Accountants**
  60 Revere Drive, Northbrook, IL 60062
  P 800-326-2163   F 847-480-9282   www.aswa.org

- **American Bar Association/ Section of Taxation**
  740 15th Street NW, Washington, DC 20005-1009
  P 202-662-8670   F 202-662-8682   www.abanet.org/tax/home.html

- **Social Security Administration**
  P 202-512-1800   F 202-512-2264   www.ssa.gov/service.html

- **Bureau of the Public Debt**
  Values and Yields for Series E/ EE Savings Bonds
  www.publicdebt.treas.gov/sav/sber1198.htm

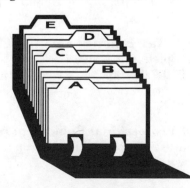

RECOMMENDED OTHER LOCAL SERVICE PROVIDERS...

- **Volunteers In Service To America (VISTA)**
  1201 New York Avenue NW, Washington, DC 20525
  P 202-606-5000   www.cns.gov/americorps/index.html

- **Service Core of Retired Executives (SCORE)**
  409 3rd Street SW, Washington, DC 20024
  P 800-634-0245   www.score.org

- **Local Small Business Development Centers (SBDCs)**
  3108 Columbia Pike, Arlington, VA 22204
  P 703-271-8700   F 703-271-8701   www.asbdc-us.org

- **Area Agency on Aging**
  www.aoa.dhhs.gov/agingsites/state.html
  P 800-677-1116

NATIONAL TAXPAYER AND RESEARCH ORGANIZATIONS

- **Citizens for Tax Justice**
  1311 L Street NW, Washington DC, 20005
  P 202-626-3780   F 202-638-3486   www.cti.org

- **The Cato Institute**
  1000 Massachusetts Ave. NW, Washington DC 20001-5403
  P 202-842-0200   F 202-842-3490   www.cato.org

- **The Foundation of Economic Education**
  30 South Broadway, Irvington, NY 10533
  P 914-591-7230   F 914-591-8910   www.fee.org

- **Better Way USA**
  PO Box 80248, Portland, OR 97280
  P 800-255-1904   www.noirs.com

- **The Brookings Institution**
  17775 Massachusetts Ave. NW, Washington DC 20036
  P 202-797-6000   F 202-797-6004   www.brook.edu

- **The Tax Foundation**
  1250 H Street NW, Washington DC 20005
  P 202-783-2760   www.taxfoundation.org

- **Americans for Tax Reform**
  1920 L Street NW, Washington DC 20006
  P 202-785-0266   F 202-785-0261   www.atr.org

- **Citizens for Limited Taxation & Government**
  PO Box 408, Peabody, MA 01960
  P 508-384-0100   //cltg.org

- **National Taxpayers Union**
  108 N. Alfred Street, Alexandria, VA 22314
  www.ntu.org

- **Taxpayers for Common Sense**
  651 Pennsylvania Avenue SE, Washington DC 20003
  P 800-TAXPAYER   F 202-546-8511   www.taxpayer.net

- **Americans for Fair Taxation**
  PO Box 27487, Houston, TX 77227
  P 888-STOP-1040   www.fairtax.org

- **Seniors Against Federal Extravagance**
  2124 Brandywood Drive, Wilmington, DE 19810
  P 302-475-7060   www.s-a-f-e.org

- **Canadian Taxpayers Federation**
  #105-438 Victoria Avenue East, Regina, Sask. S4N ON7
  P 800-667-7933   F 800-465-4464   www.taxpayer.com

Develop A Three-Year Plan

	Year	Year	Year

Objective: Percent Tax Reduction _____ _____ _____

Category	Plan	Impact

Income
- Family Splitting _____
- Delaying _____
- _____ _____

Deductible Expenses
- Scheduling _____
- Charitable _____
- _____ _____

Education
- Saving _____
- College _____
- Continuing _____

Retirement Planning
- IRA Saving _____
- _____ _____

Tax Shelters
- Real Estate _____
- _____ _____

Investing
- Tax-Free _____
- Sell/Buy Assets _____

Self-Employment
- Start Business _____
- Home Office _____
- _____ _____

Credits
- _____ _____

Important Phone Numbers and Addresses...

Accountant:
Name _____
Address _____
Phone/Fax _____
References _____

Banker:
Name _____
Address _____
Phone/Fax _____
References _____

Lawyer:
Name _____
Address _____
Phone/Fax _____
References _____

Employer:
Name _____
Address _____
Phone/Fax _____
References _____

Insurance Broker:
Name _____
Address _____
Phone/Fax _____
References _____

_____:
Name _____
Address _____
Phone/Fax _____
References _____

THE ALL-PURPOSE DEDUCTION TRACKING FORM

Instruction: Use this form to track a miscellaneous deductible expense type that you incur periodically over the course of year.

Deduction Type:_____

Deduction	Date	Reference	Reason/Notes/Supplier	Amount

Example: *Investments*

Software	*2/3/00*	*Check #1011*	*Investing Support/Intuit*	*$100.00*

Notes:

Notes:

Notes: